A Buncha Fruits!
And other deliciousities

A fun, inclusive anthropomorphic coloring book for all ages

KN Granger

DEDICATION

This volume is dedicated to anyone who enjoys curiosities and deliciousness – or, as they might be called, deliciousities!

Illustration 1: Mary Berry is a strawberry who's ready to get out of the basket and make a splash at the big picnic.

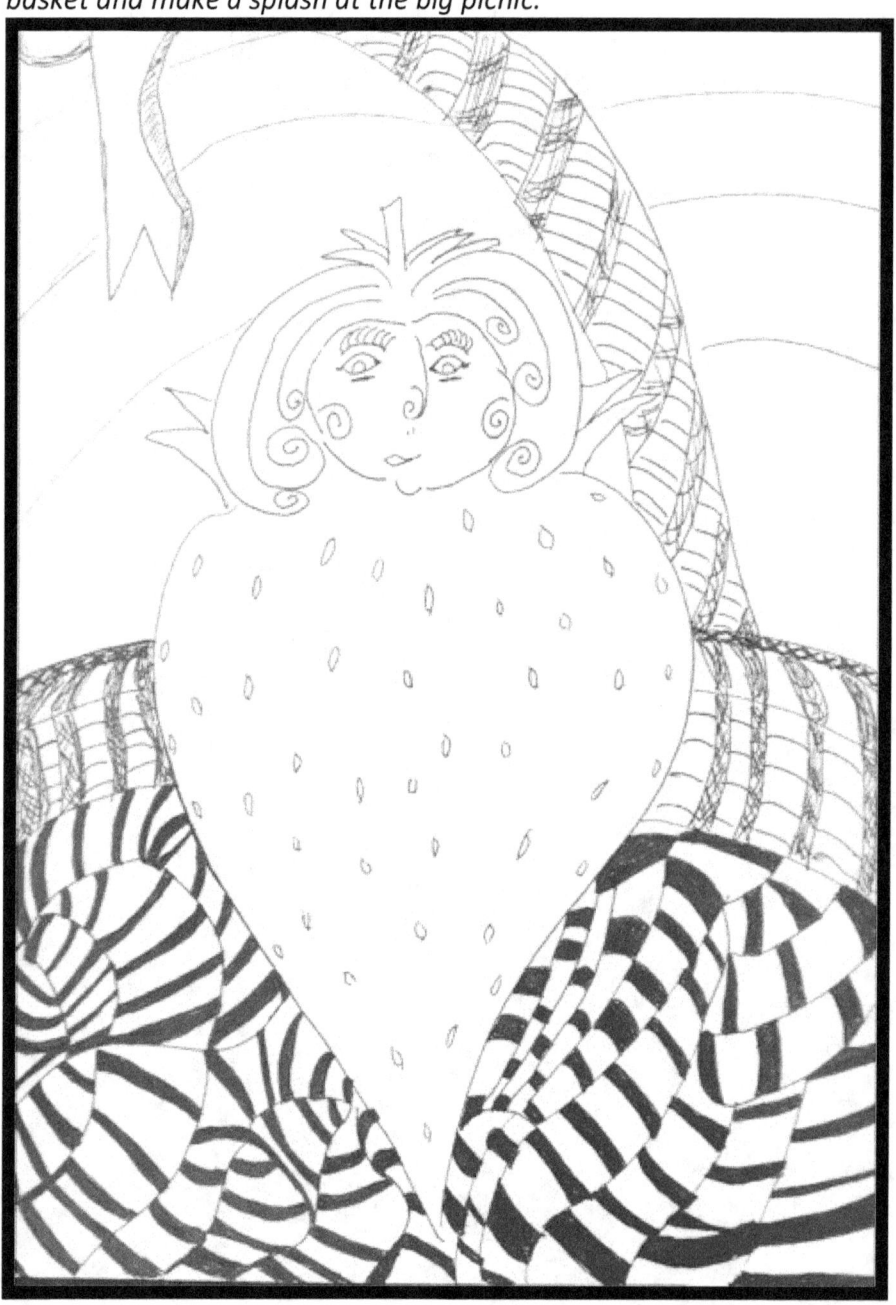

Illustration 2: Perri the Pear is just a little bit sour, but a little sunshine and honey will sweeten her right up.

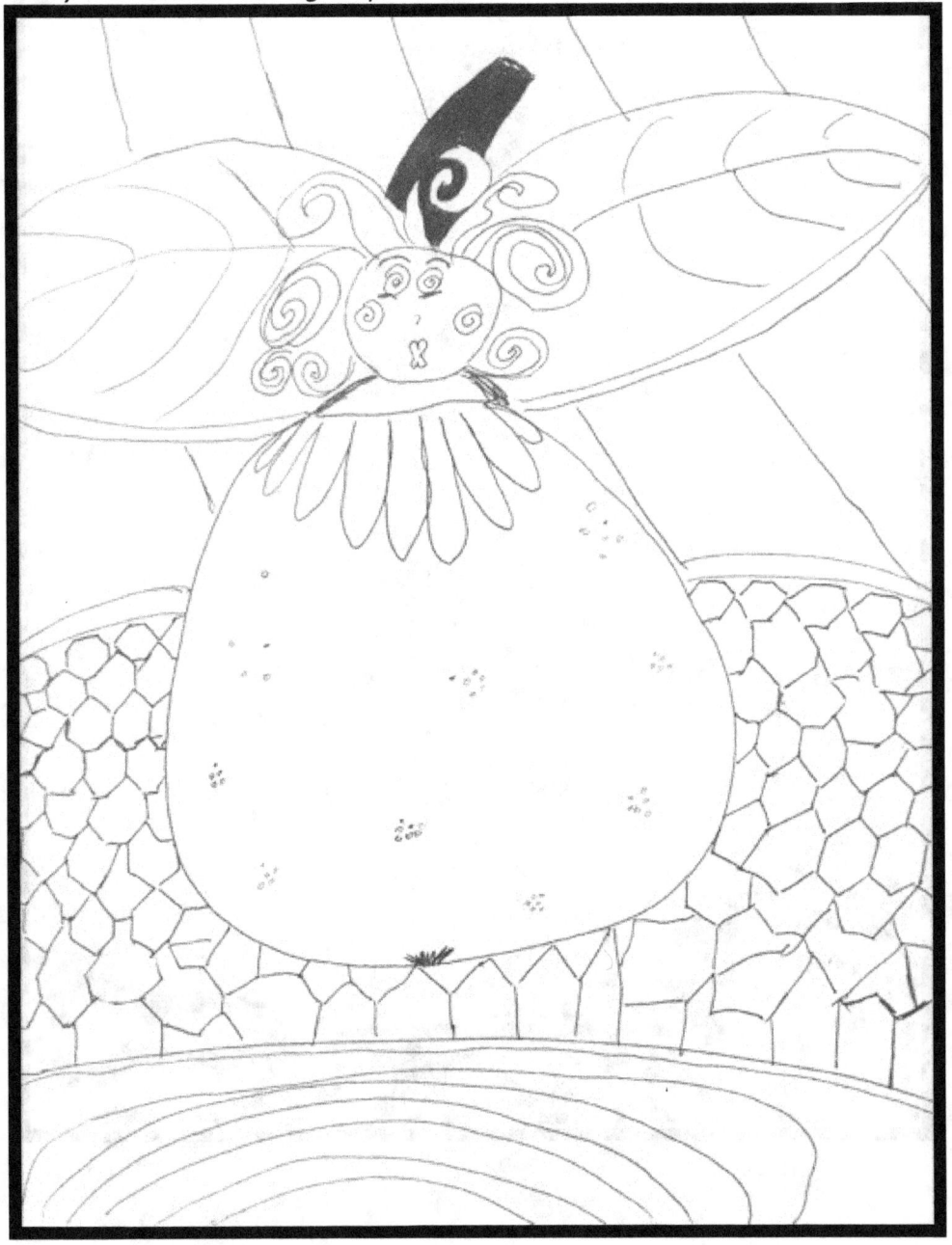

Illustration 3: Peach Pit Patty: She doesn't always get a chance to come out and share her mind, but when she does she really shines.

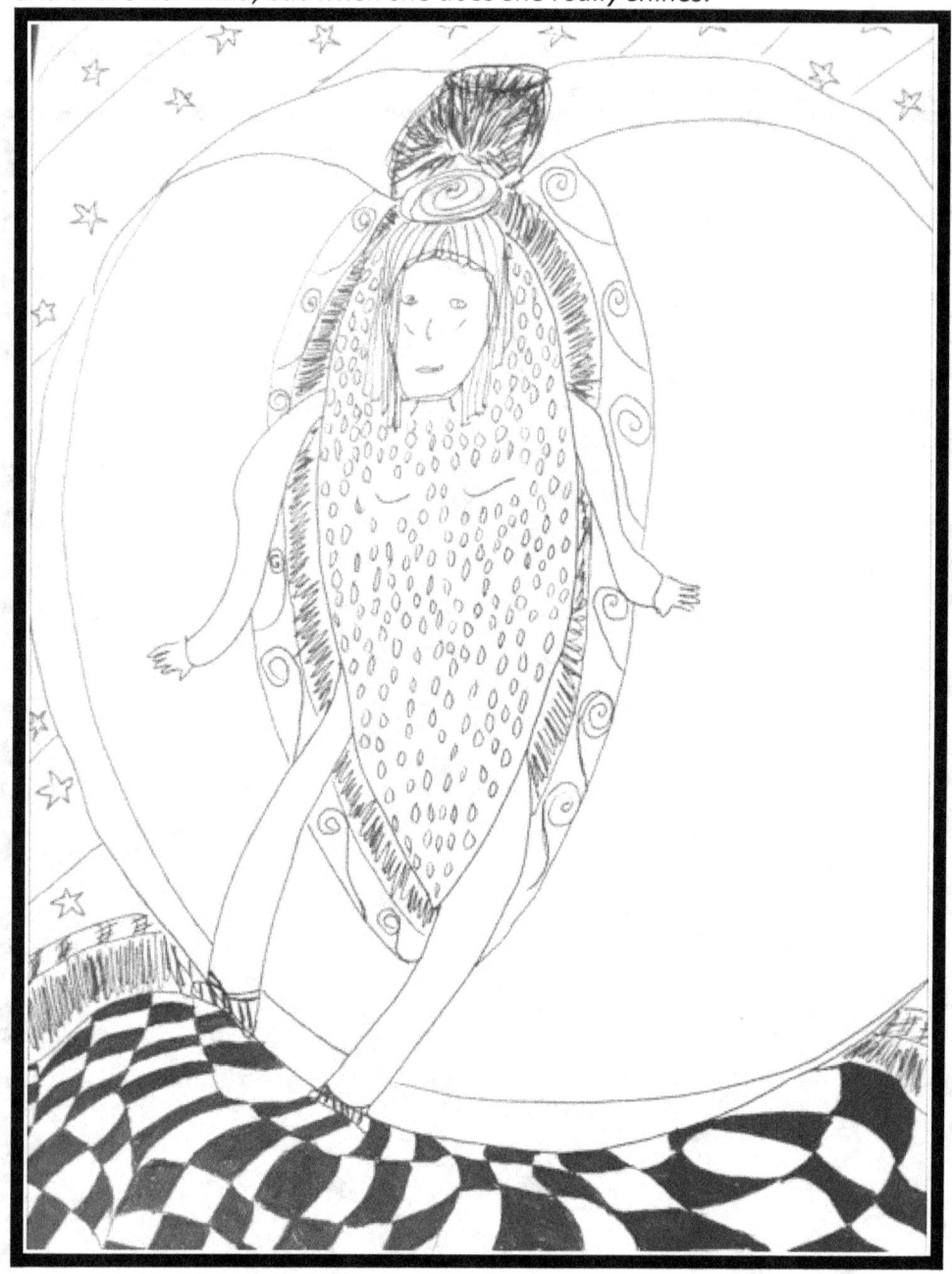

Illustration 4: Birthday Cake Bard always comes alight for a friend's special day!

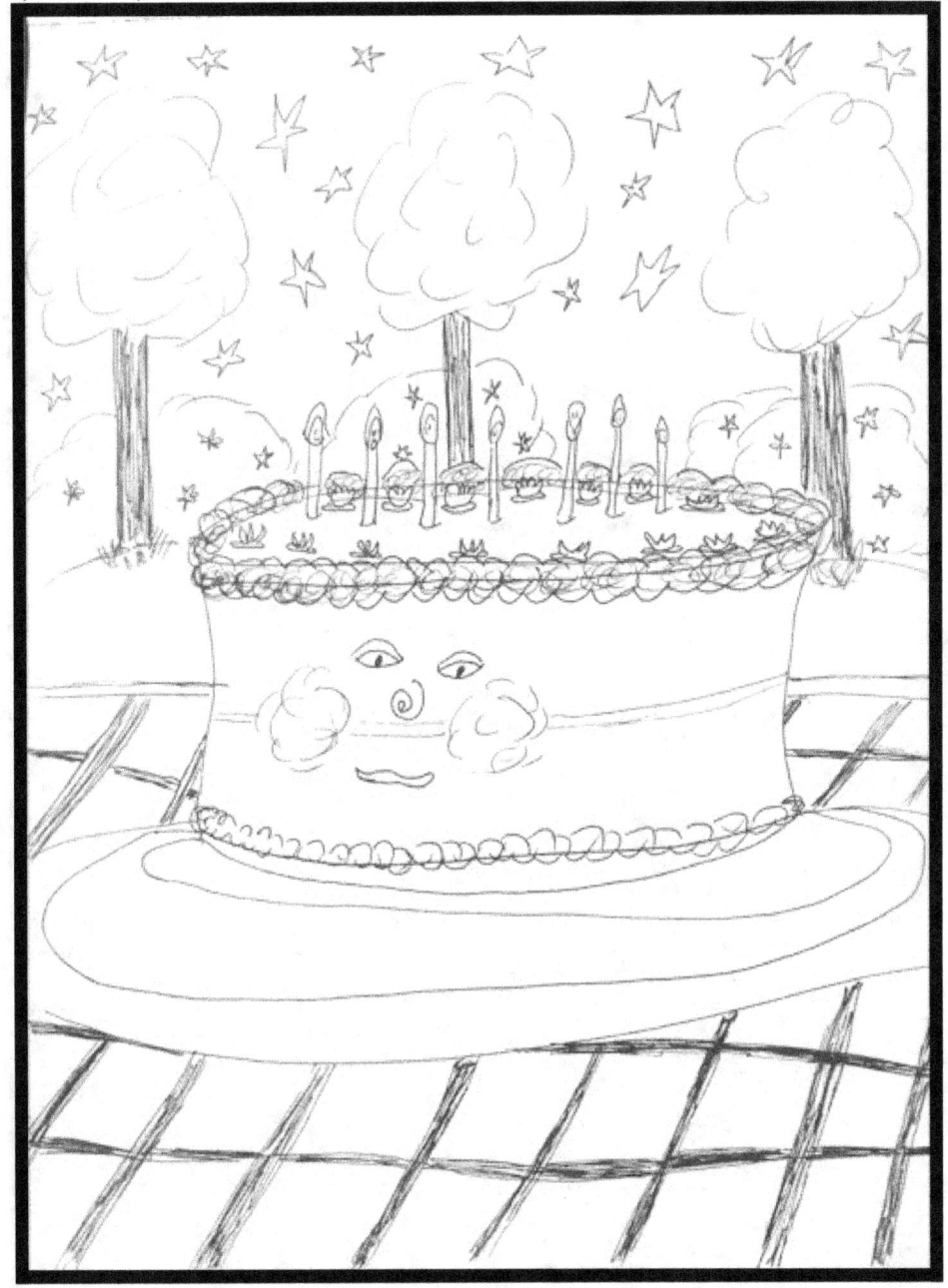

Illustration 5: Tsai the Teapot treats her little teacups with a delicate green-tea brew.

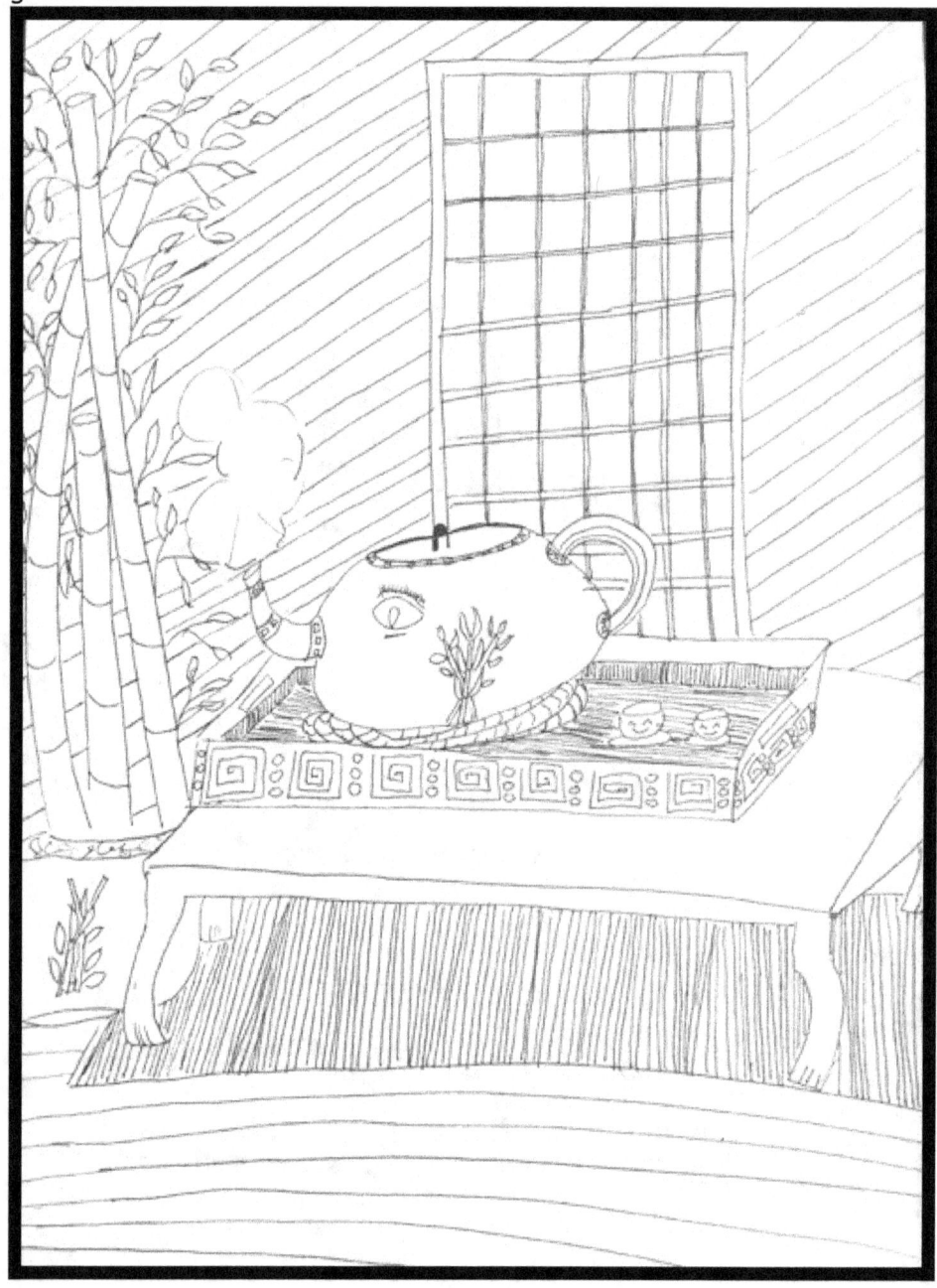

Illustration 6: Wendy the Watermelon is not too wild about this windy weather.

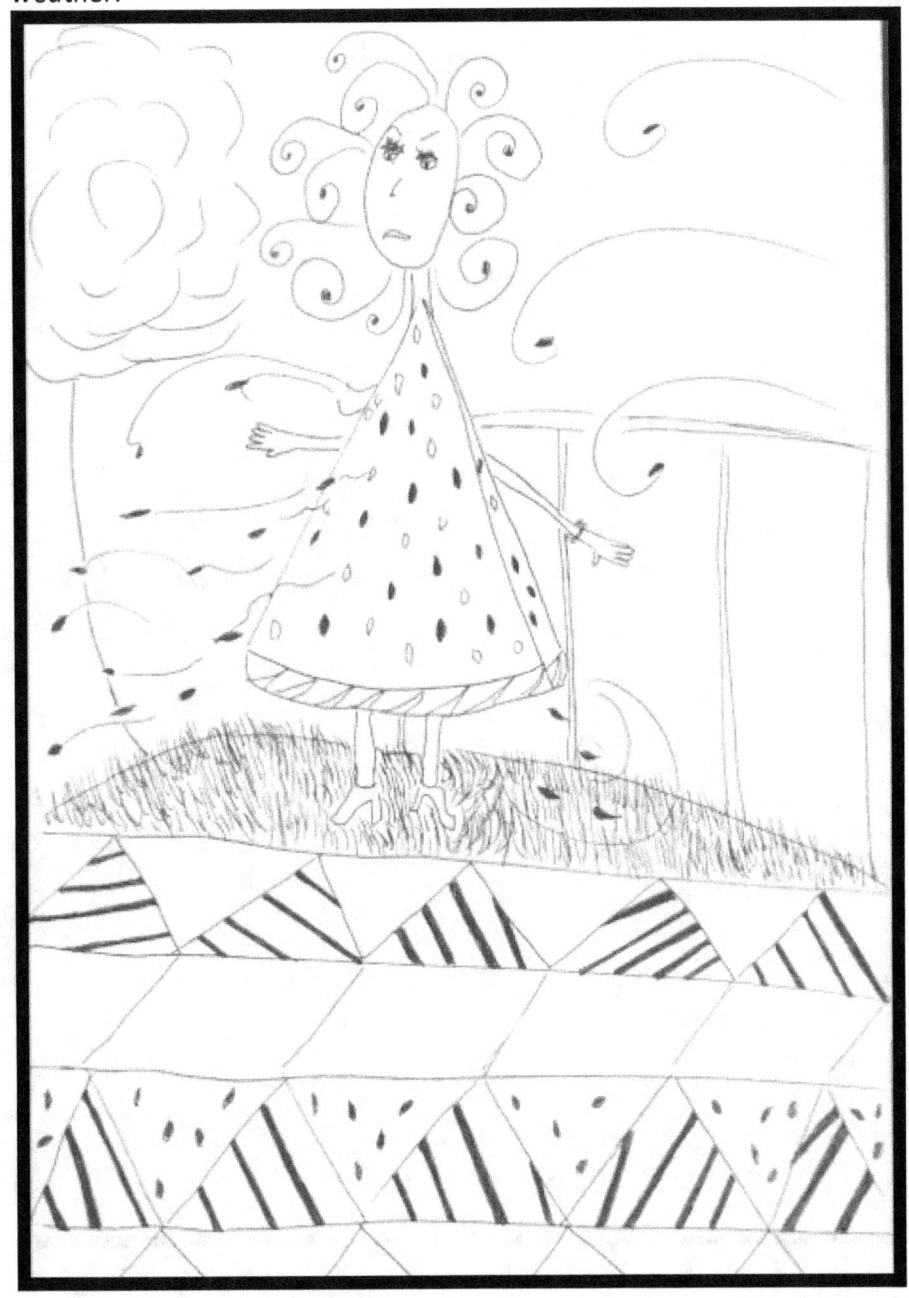

Illustration 7: Betty the blueberry listens to the blues on her boombox.

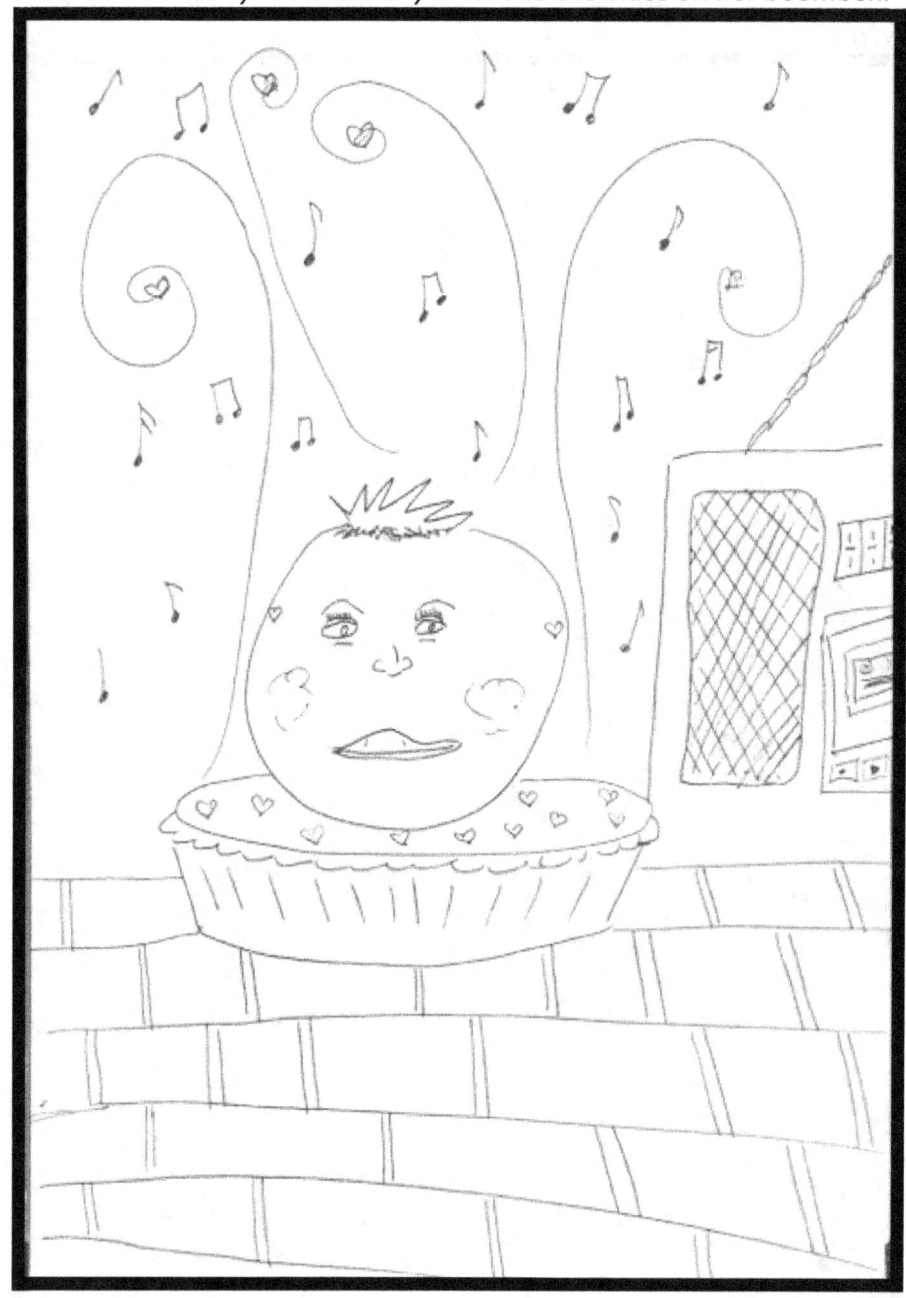

Illustration 8: All the cherries at the Discotheque Cherie are having a good time tonight.

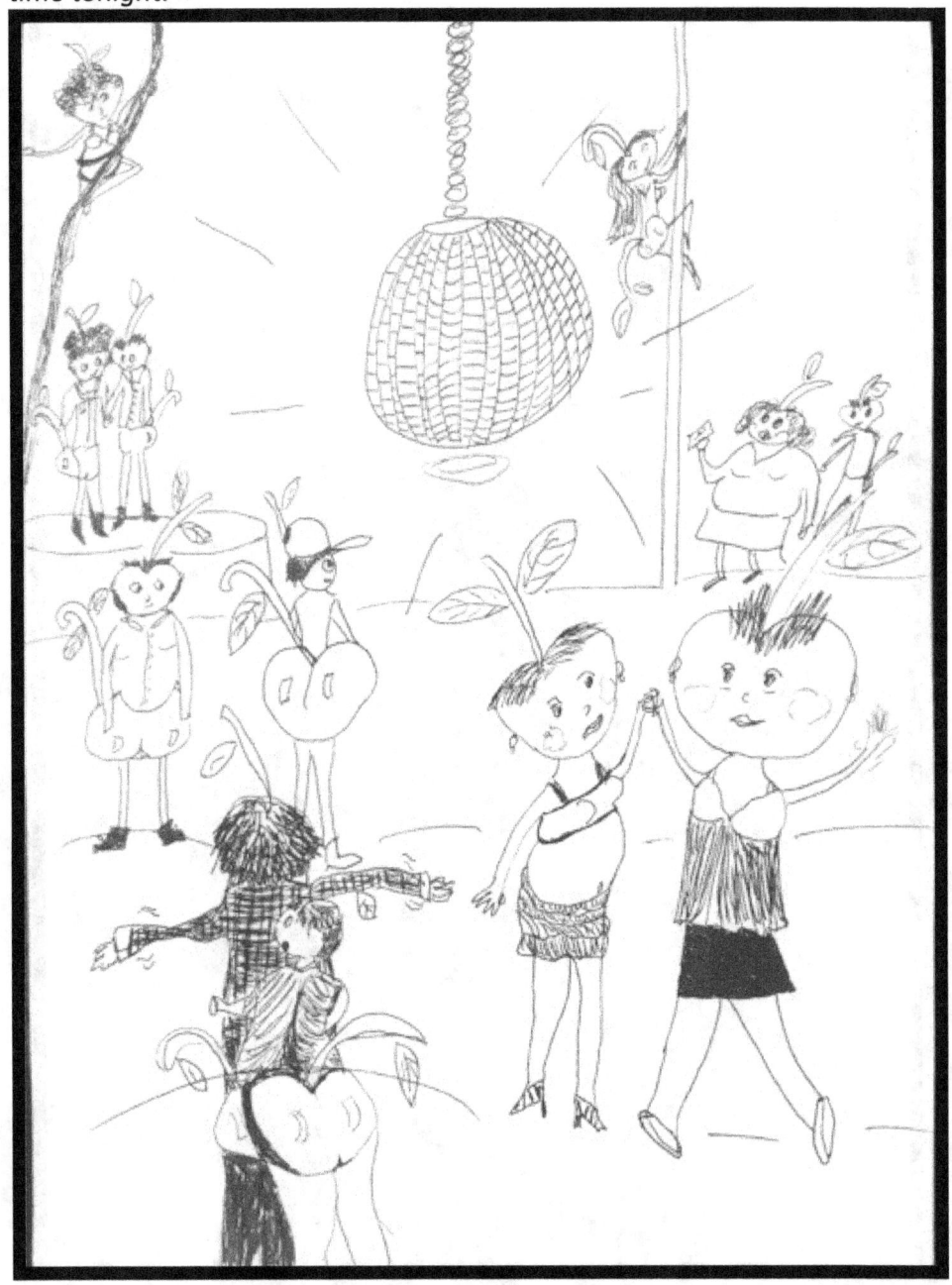

Illustration 9: Ida the Ice Cream Queen is a jolly lady who knows how to please.

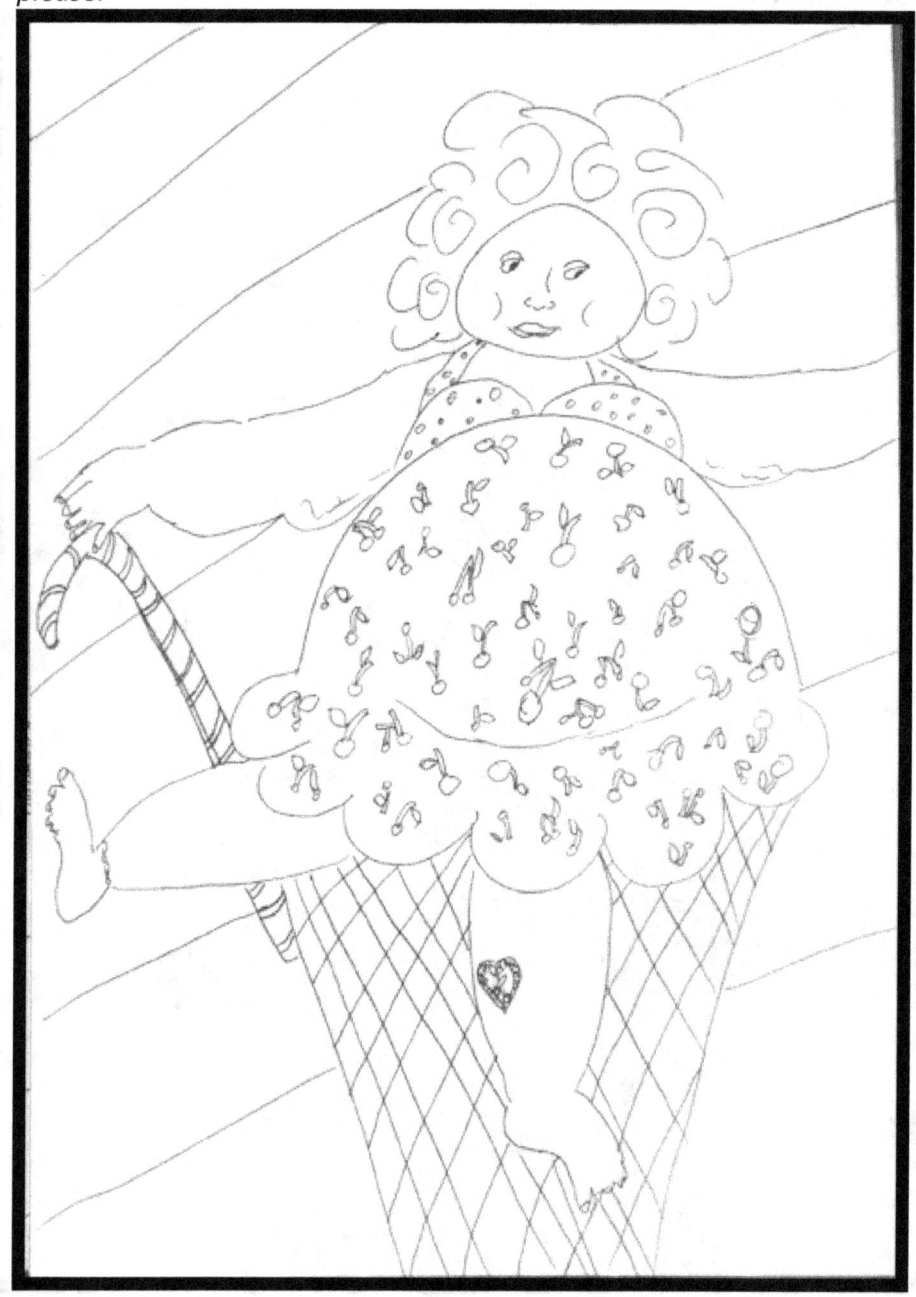

Illustration 10: Benjamin the Bagel is ready to take on the day with some fresh dill and lox!

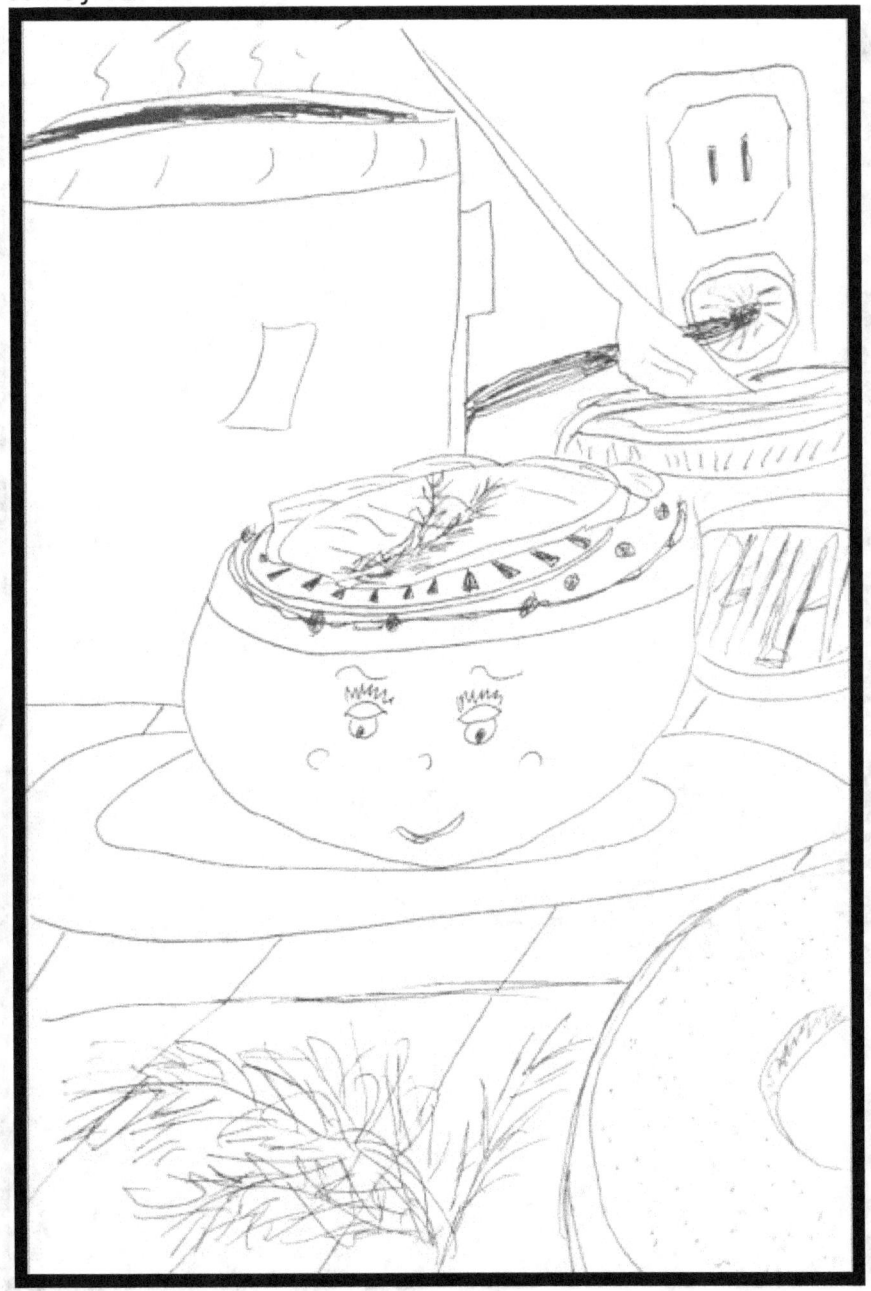

Illustration 11: Levona the Lintzer Cookie is leaning on the subway pole at the end of a long day.

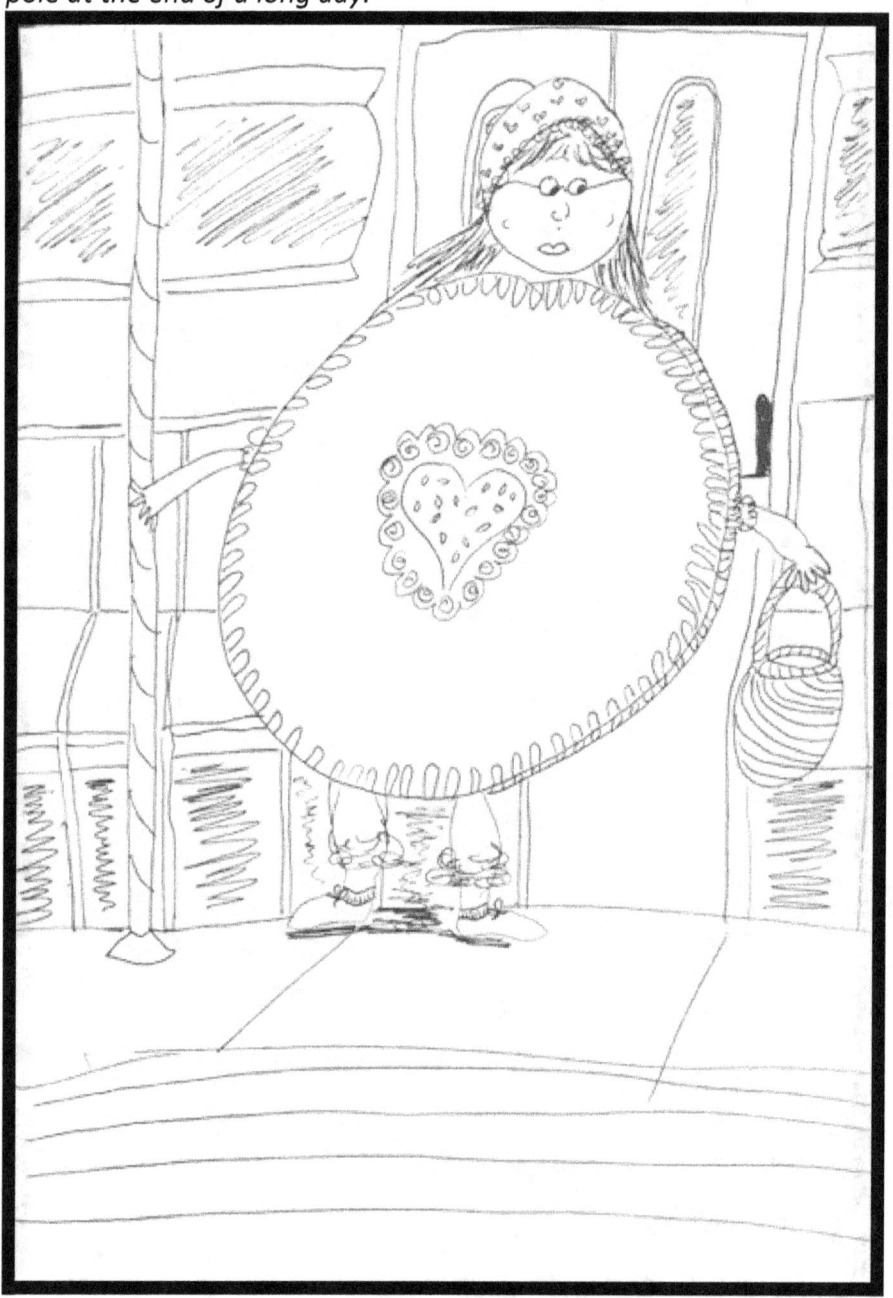

Illustration 12: The Magical Mystery Meatballs are making this meal melodious.

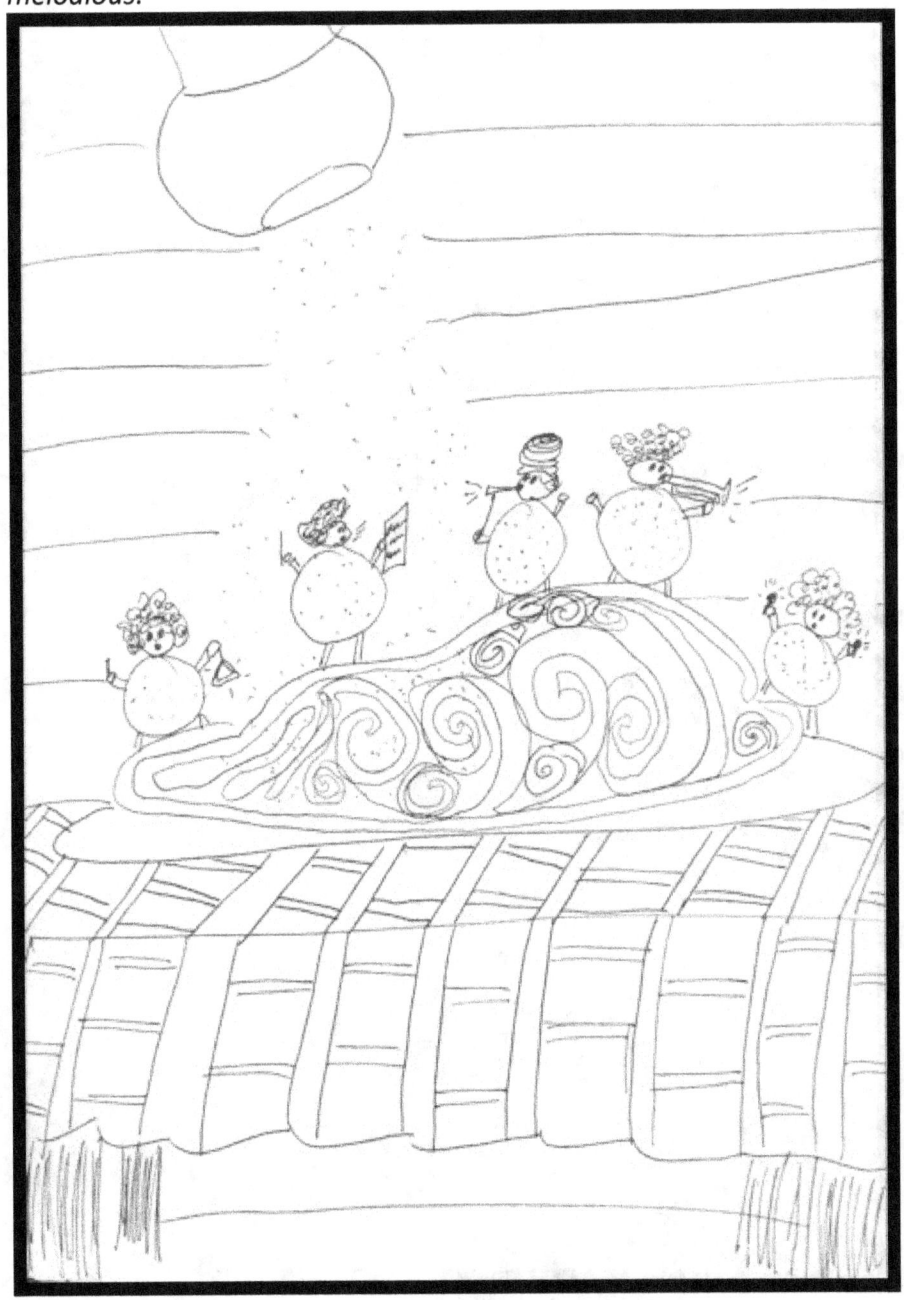

Illustration 13: Minnelli the Macaroon is making a marvelous splash in a Berlin cabaret.

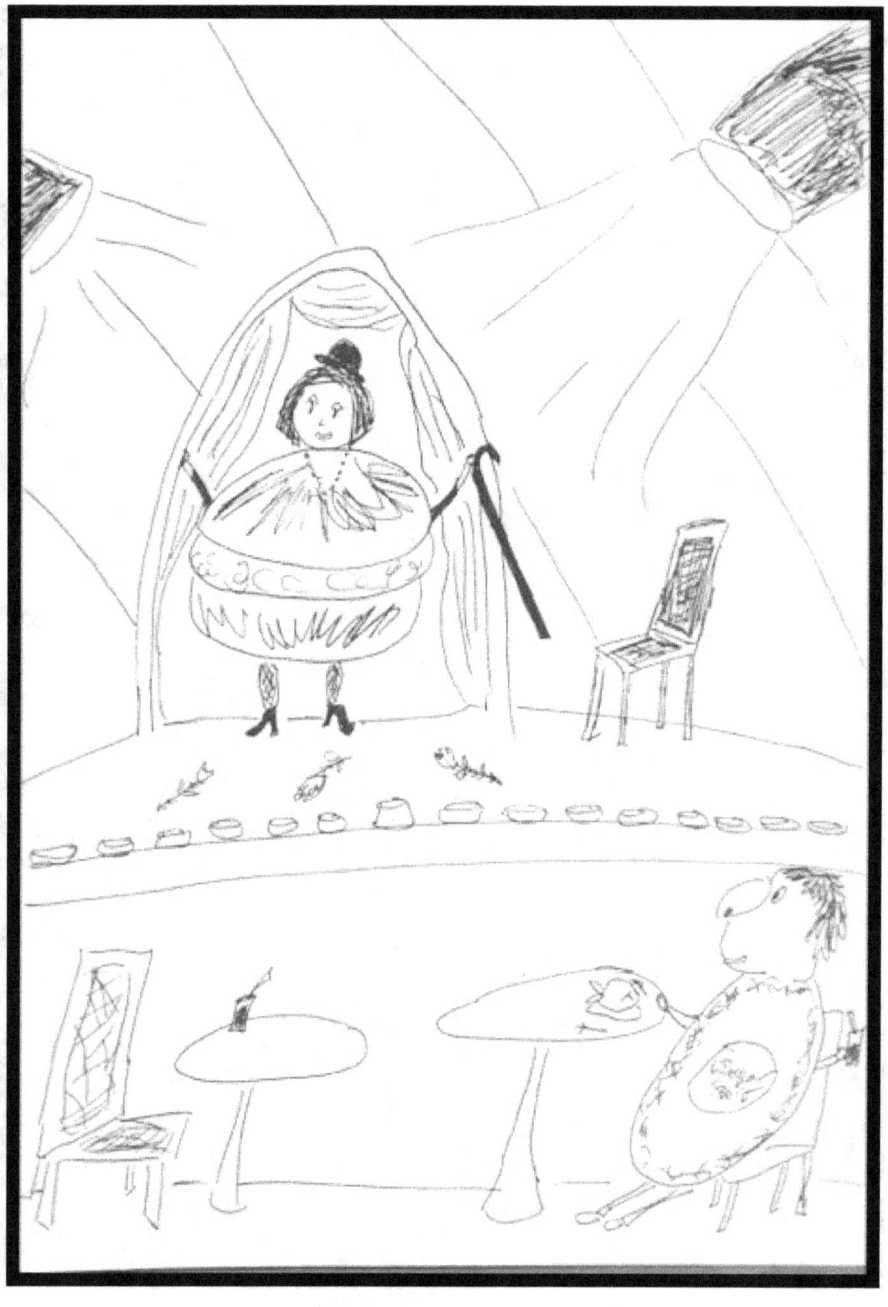

Illustration 14: Charlie the cotton candy patiently awaits someone to choose them.

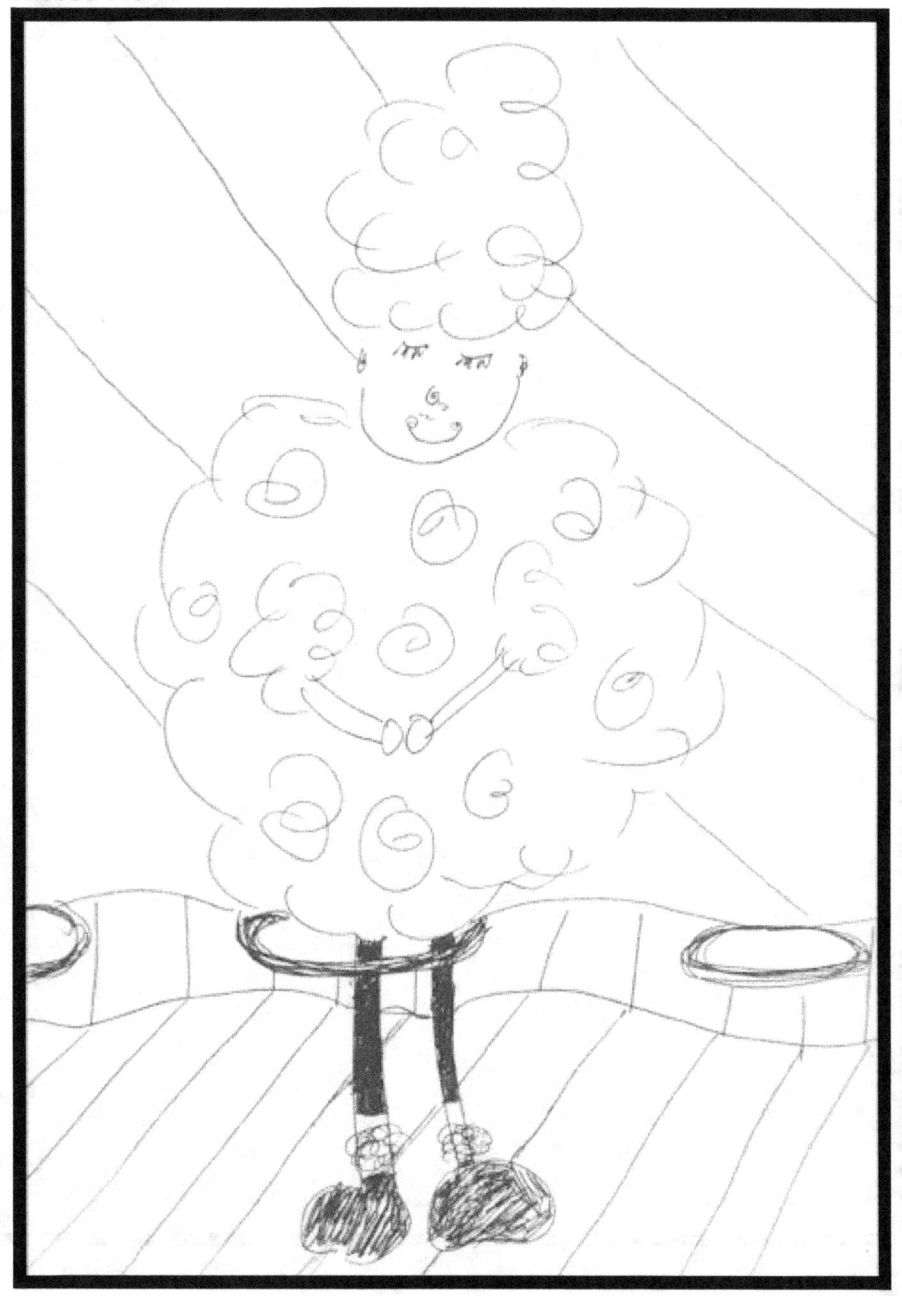

Illustration 15: Carlos the Cupcake chases the tide on the beach.

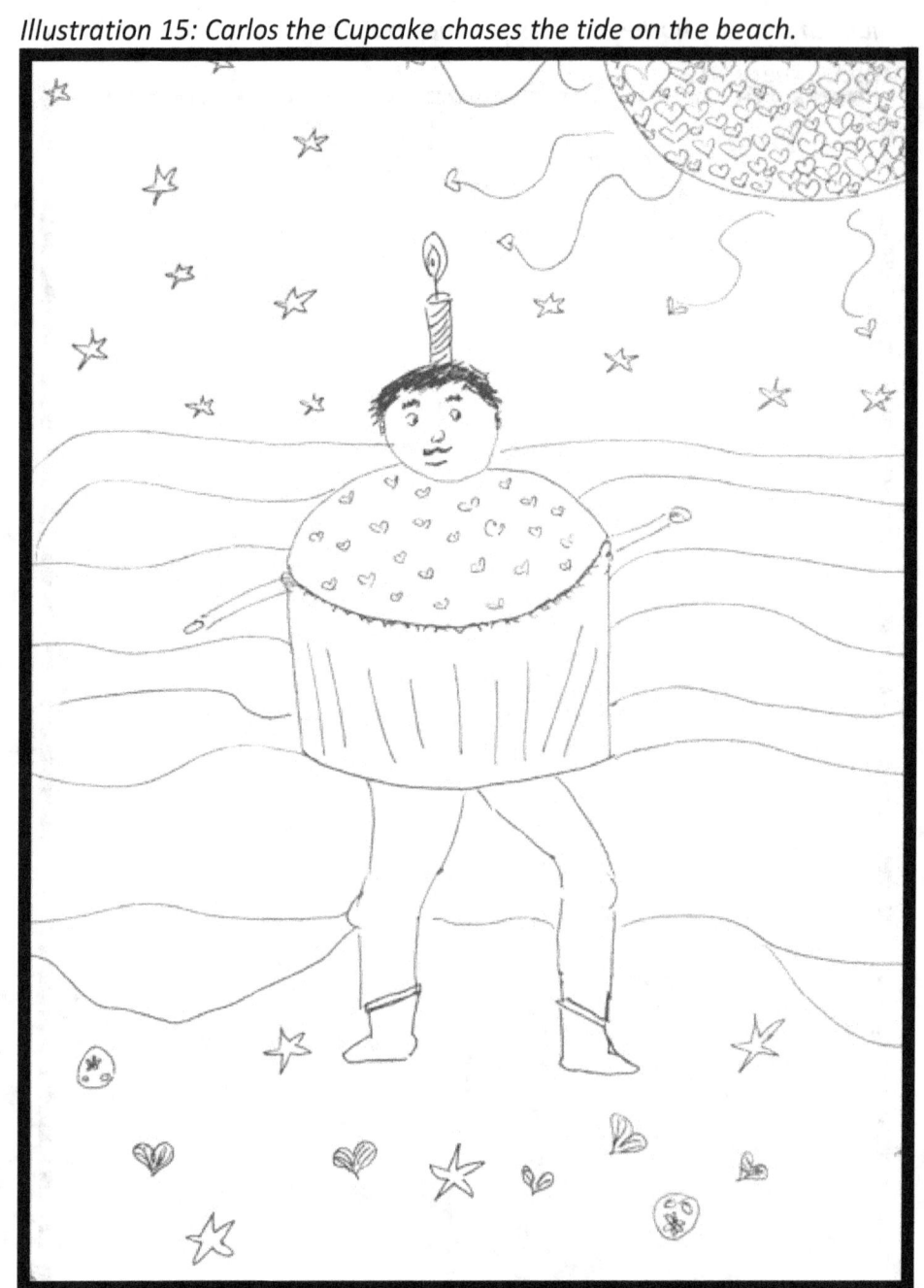

Illustration 16: Greta Grape-o gathers her thoughts in her gracious Hollywood mansion.

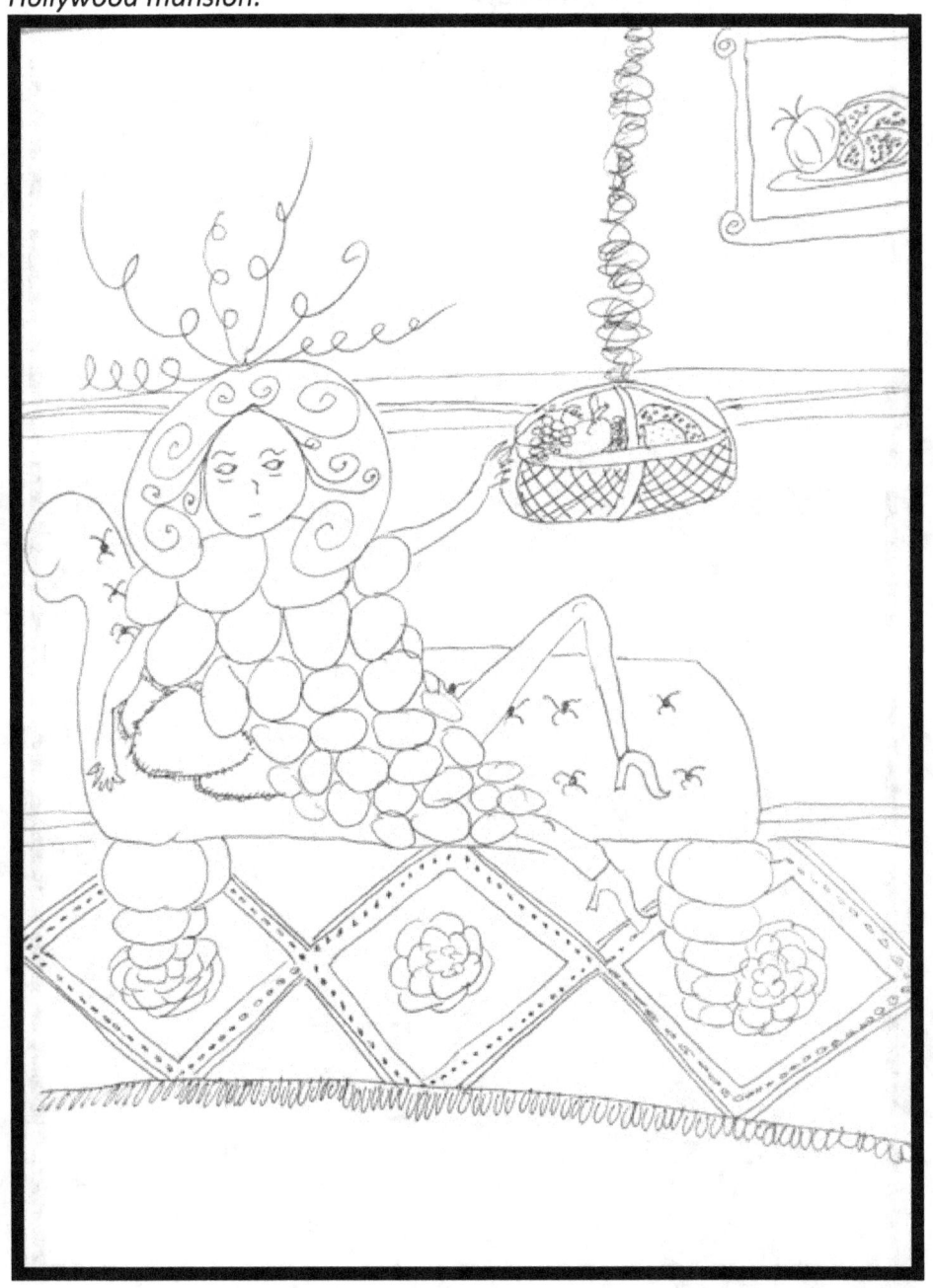

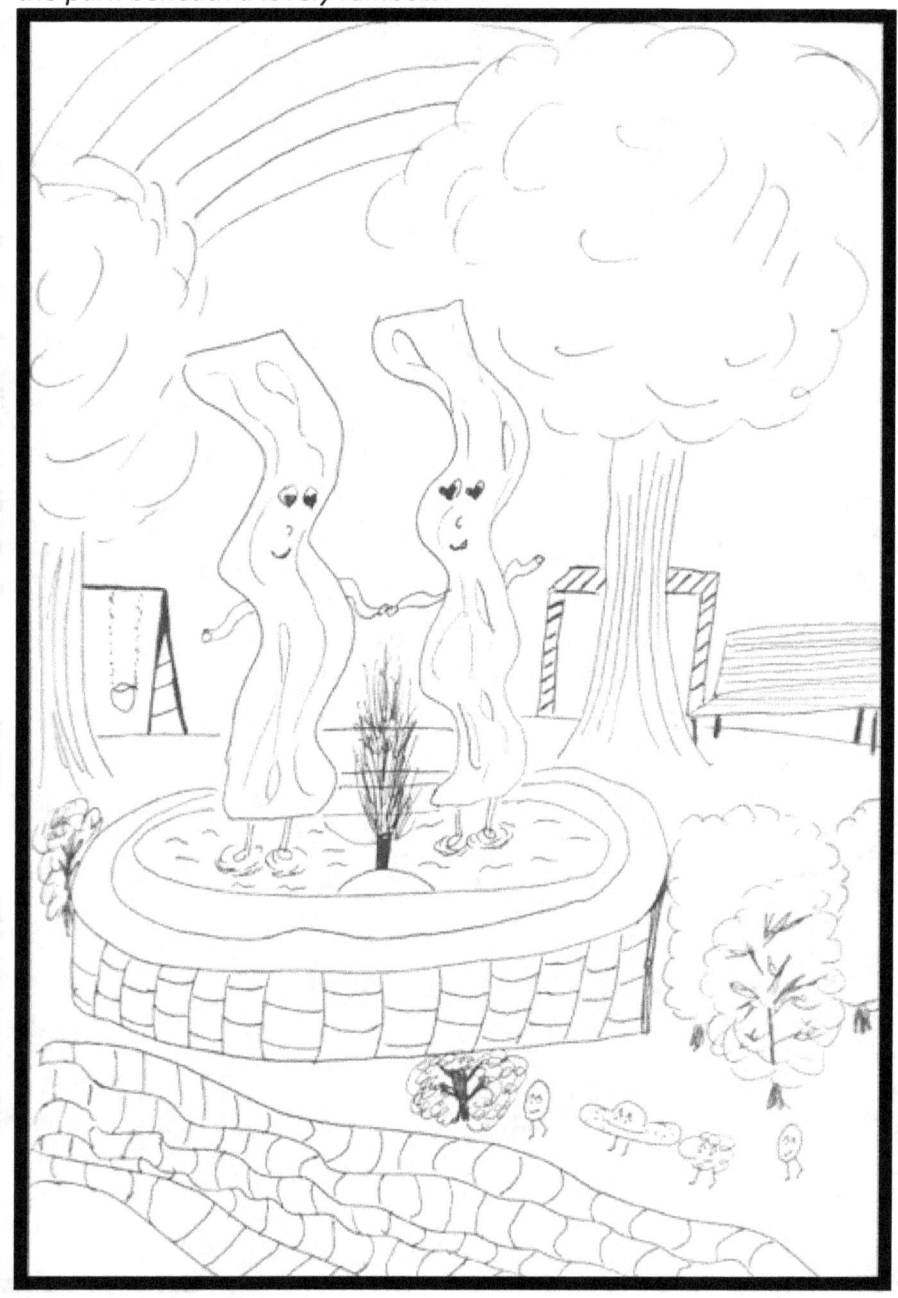

Illustration 18: Cerena the Cinnamon Roll clears her throat before her operatic crescendo.

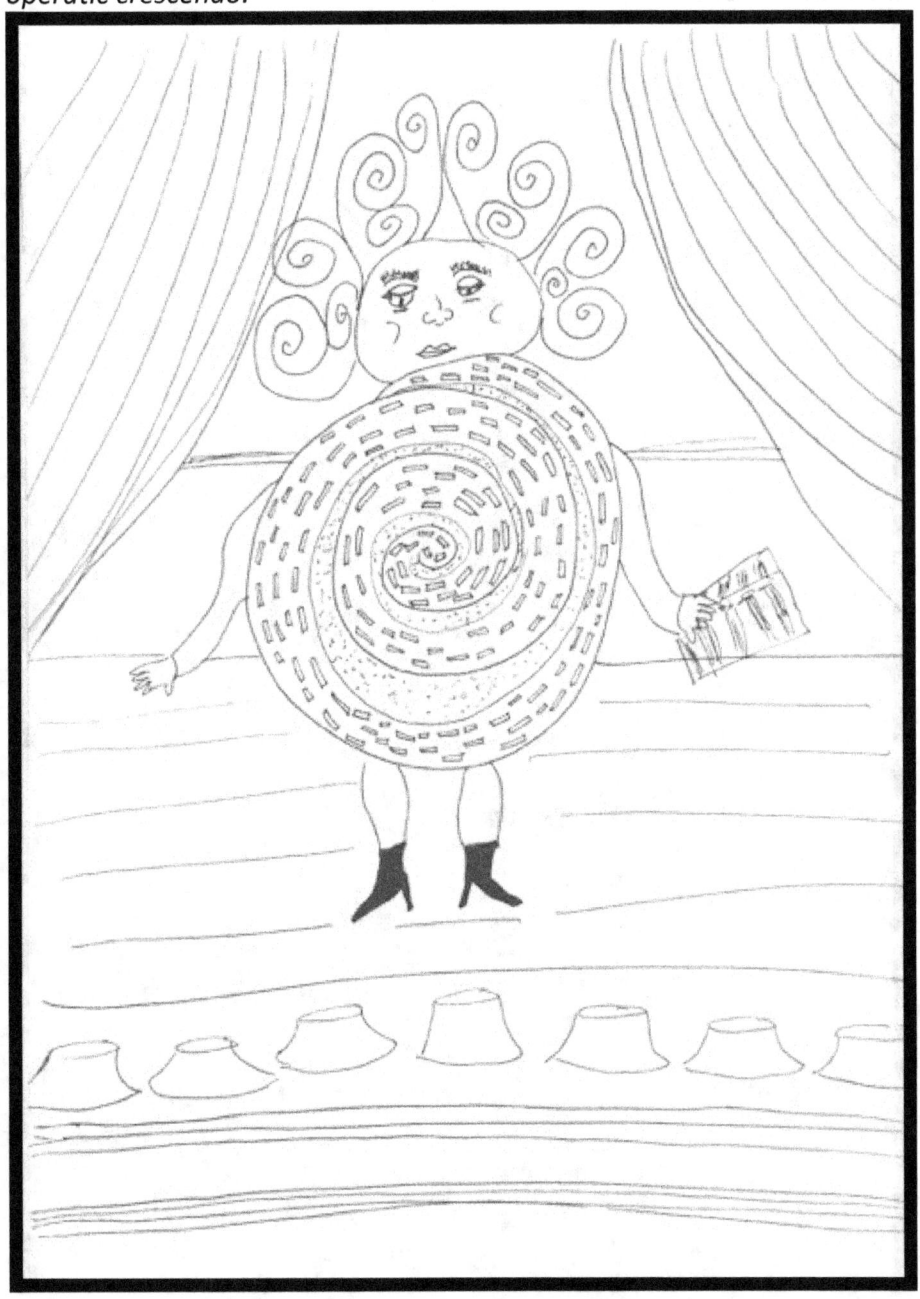

Illustration 19: Walida the Waffle-Cone wades through the waters of the candy-strewn river.

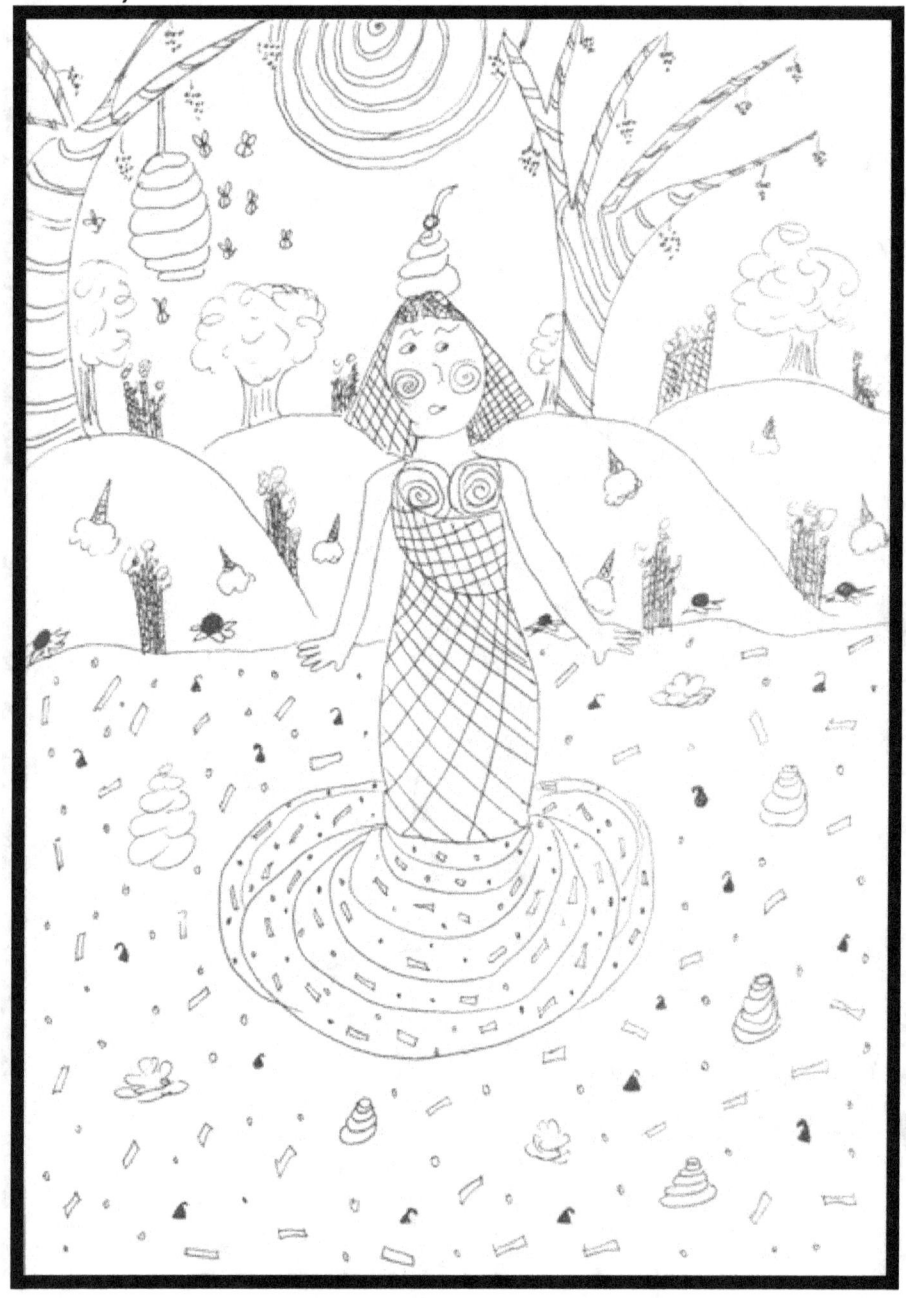

*Illustration 20: Greta and Gordie Gourd spend a quiet night in,
watching Squash and Gorder.*

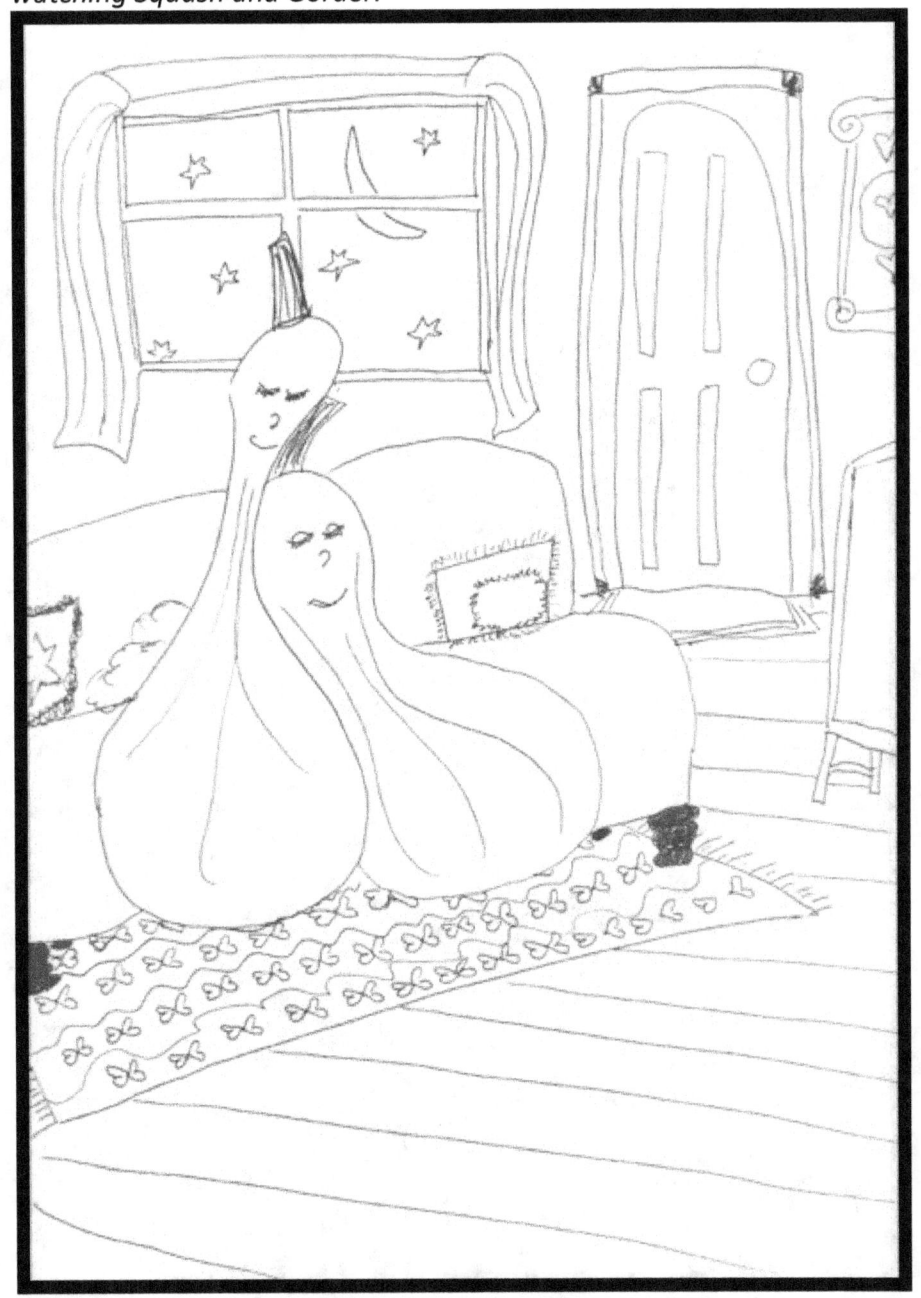

Illustration 21: B-Nama relaxes at a park while contemplating their next solo R and B album.

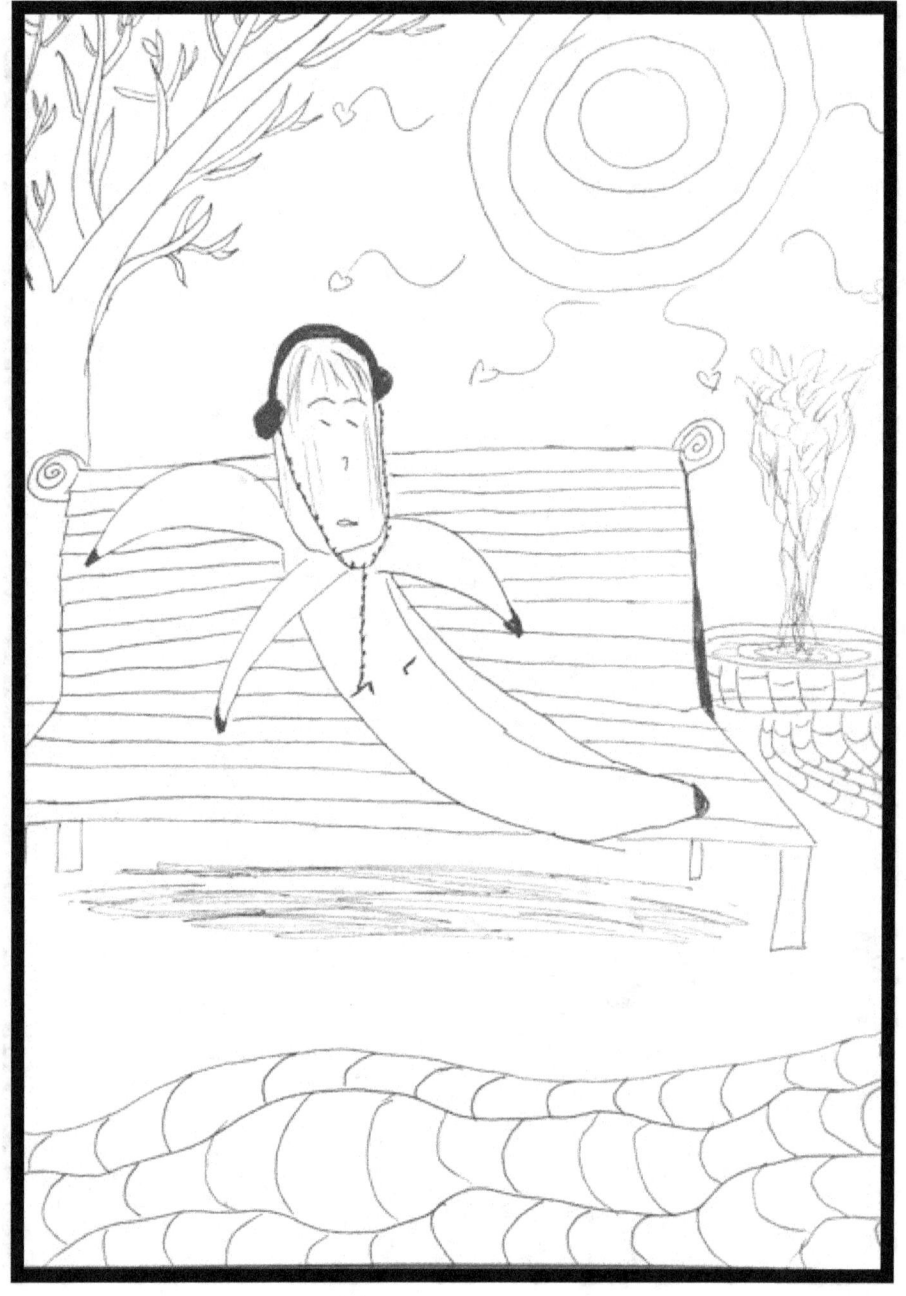

Illustration 22: Princex Pomegranate presides at the bow of their ship as they approach the shore of their kingdom.

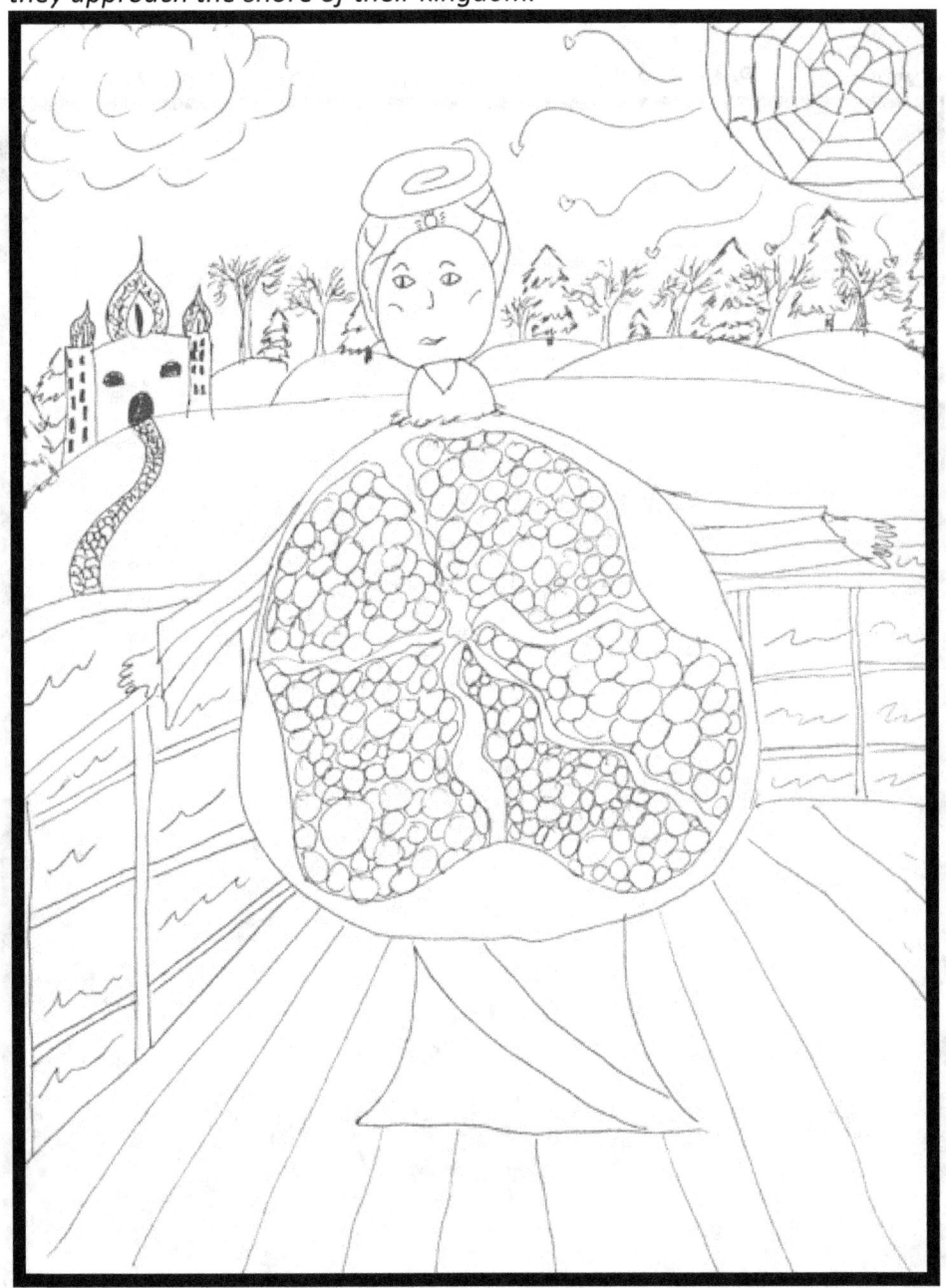

Illustration 23: Petey the Pizza luxuriates with a piece of a fresh hot pie.

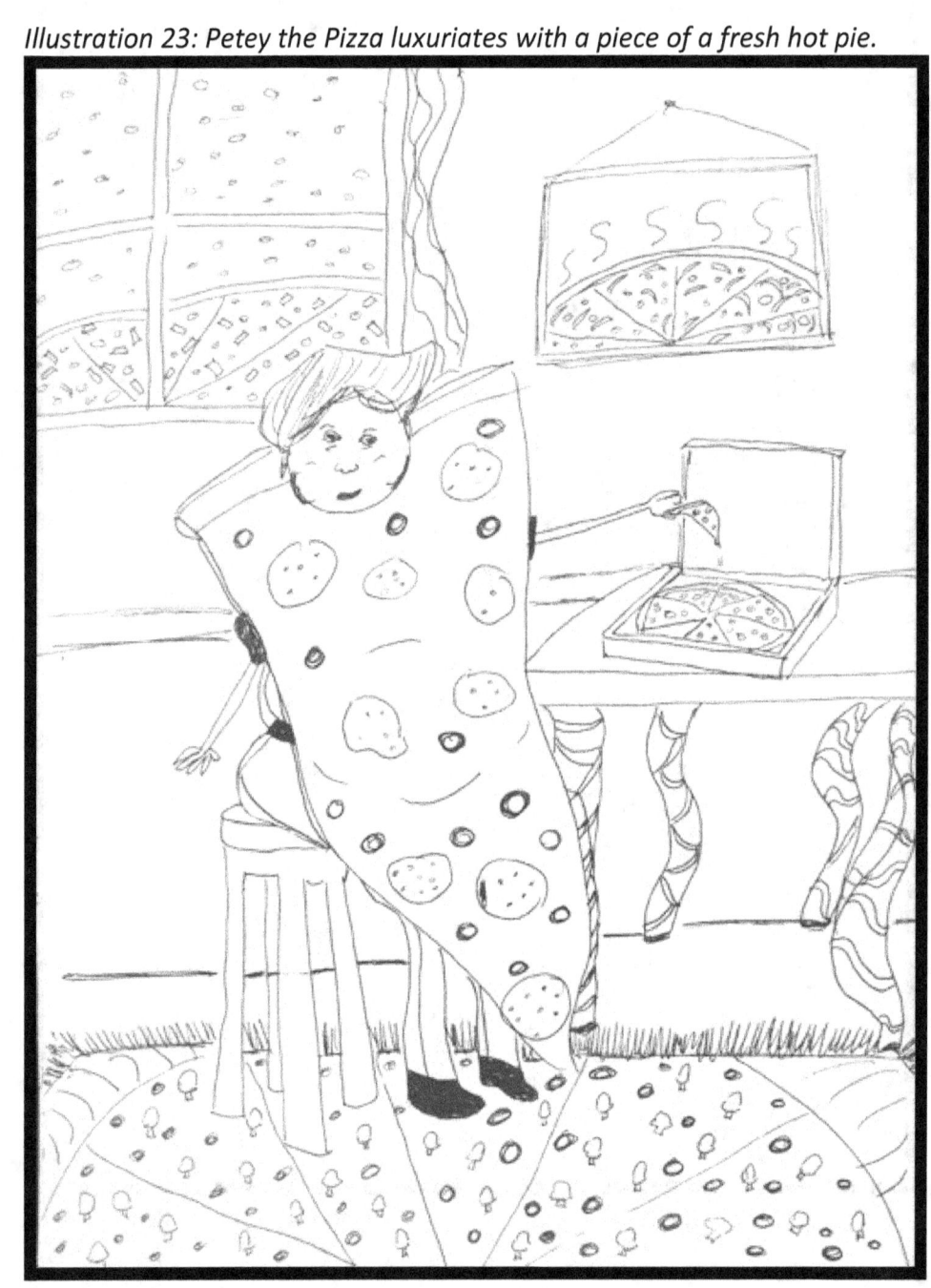

Illustration 24: Lady Saladia dances among the many radishes, olives, and tomato slices that entertain her court.

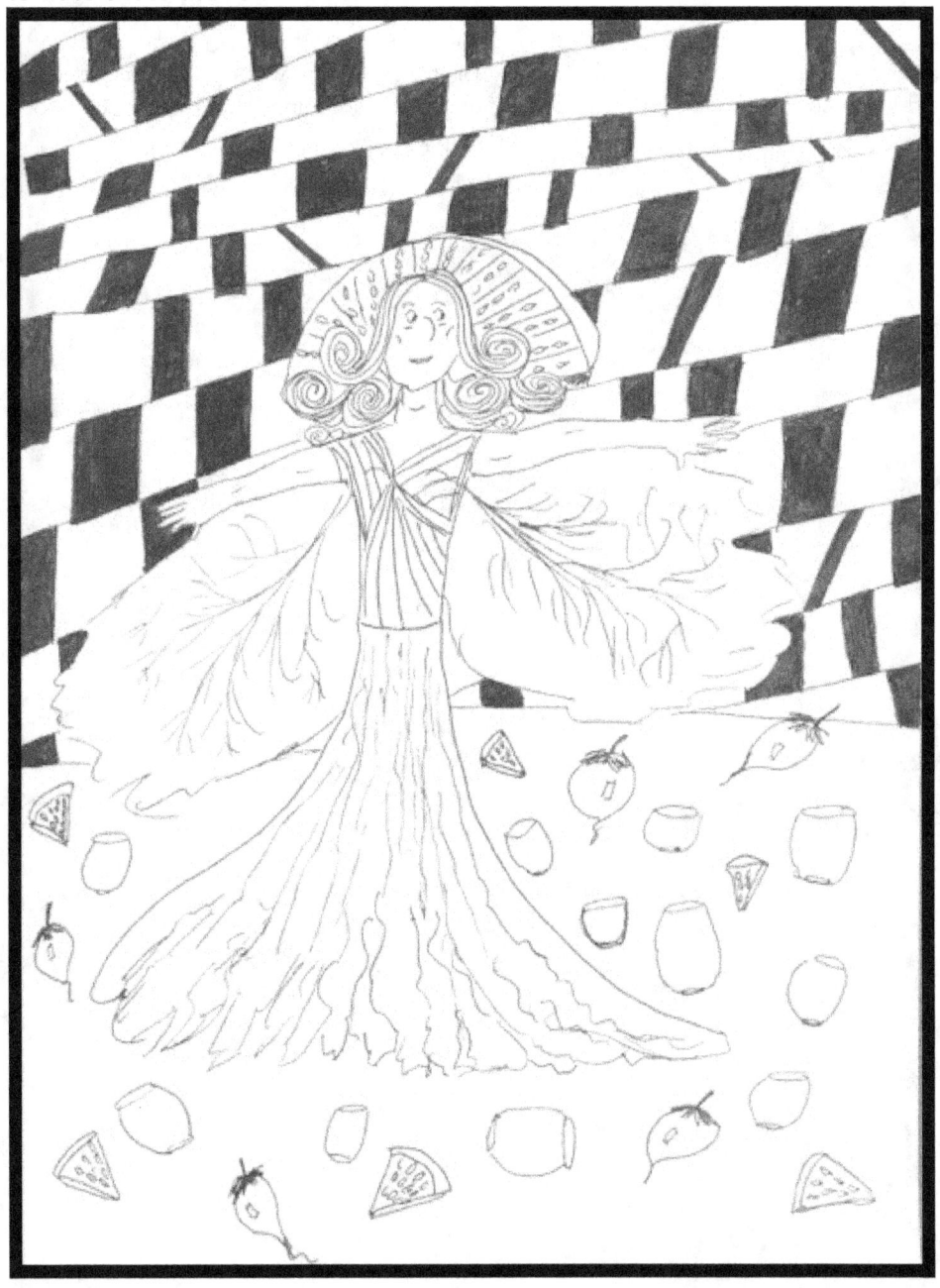

ABOUT THE AUTHOR

KN Granger is a modern polymath who lives in the Bronx, NYC and works in Westchester, NY. She has a website called RoseClue.Com where you can check out all the cool things she does. Thanks for checking out this book!

www.ingramcontent.com/pod-product-compliance
Lightning Source LLC
Chambersburg PA
CBHW081624220526
45468CB00010B/3018